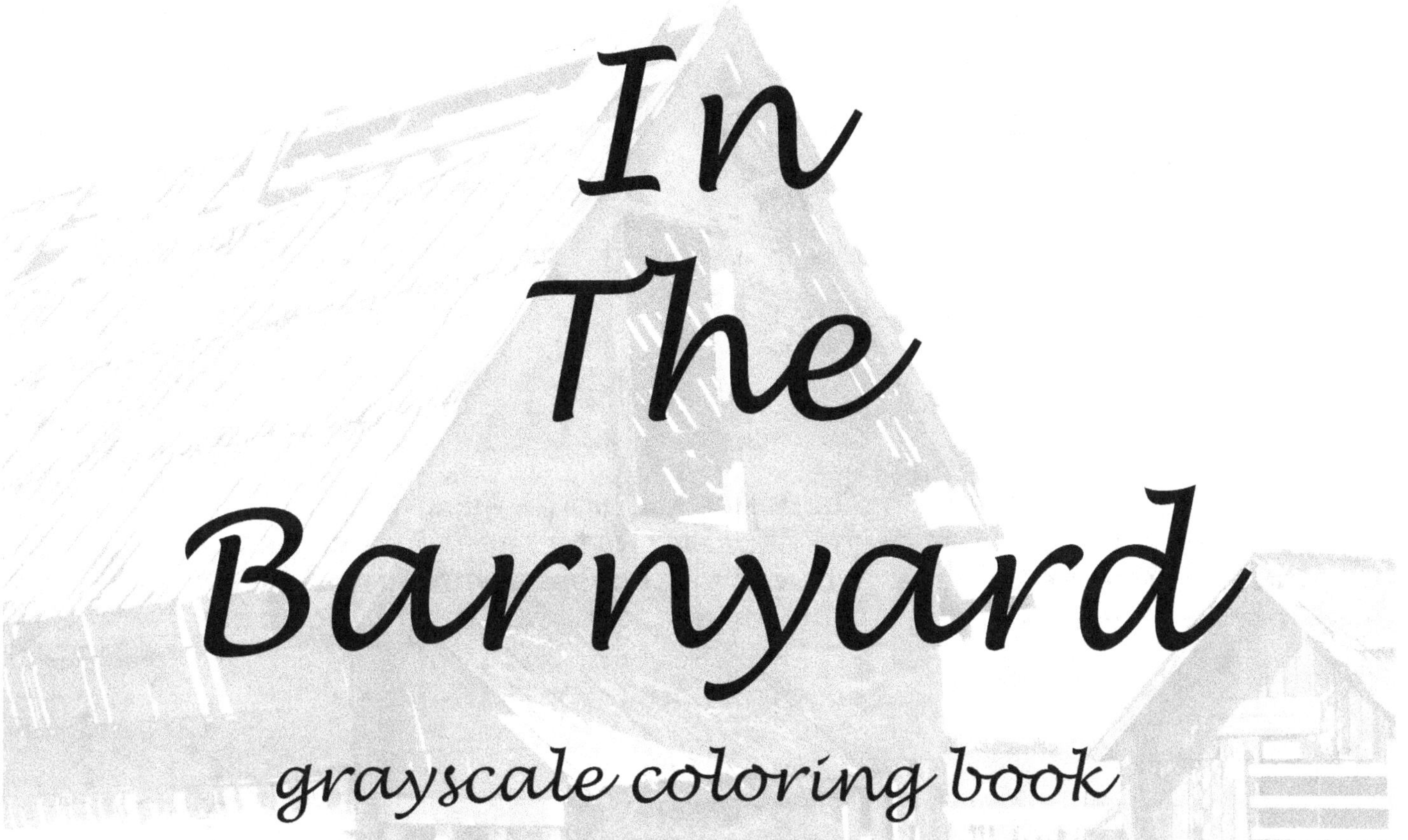

In The Barnyard

grayscale coloring book

curated by
Tabz Jones

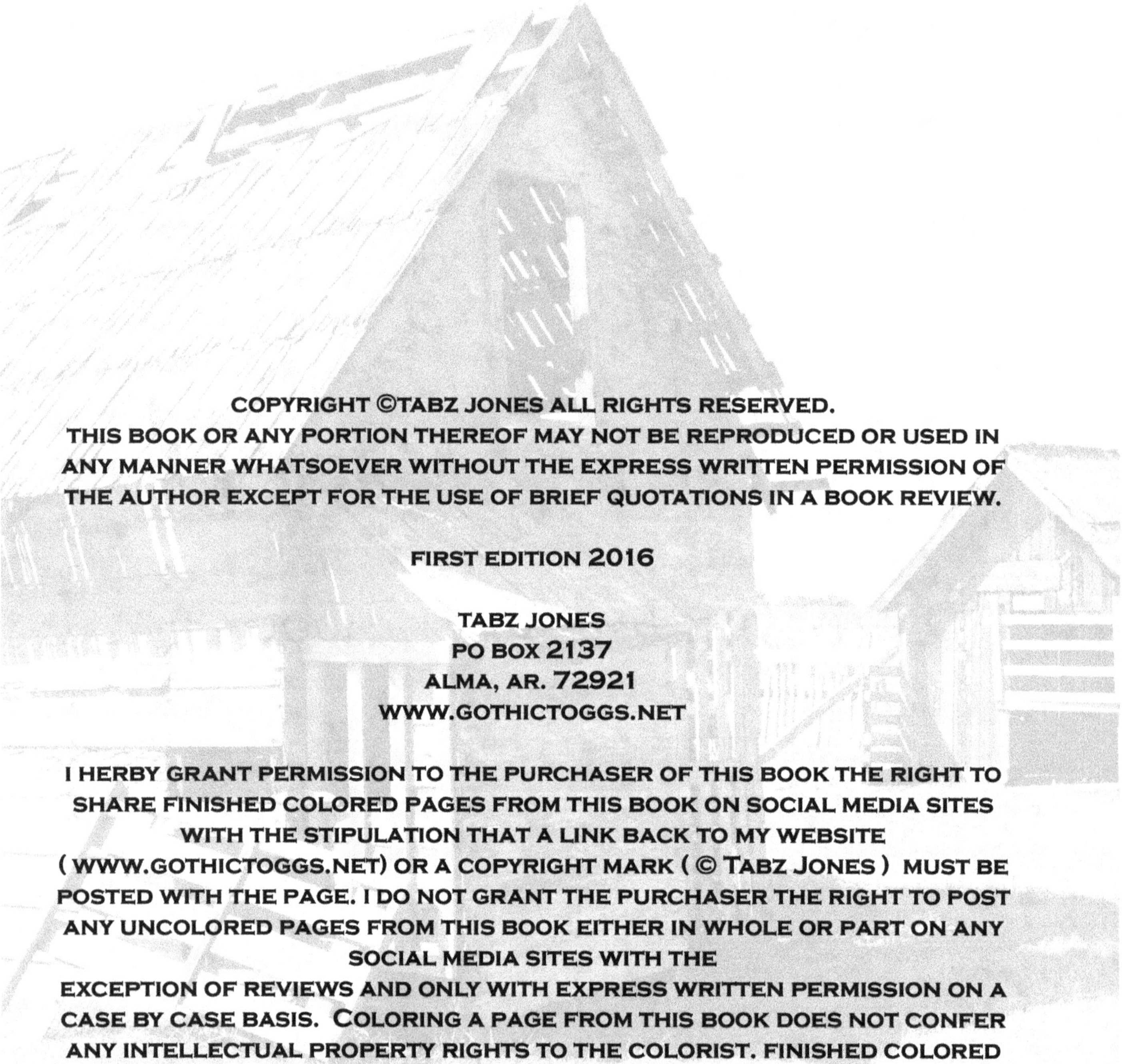

FIRST EDITION 2016

TABZ JONES
PO BOX 2137
ALMA, AR. 72921
WWW.GOTHICTOGGS.NET

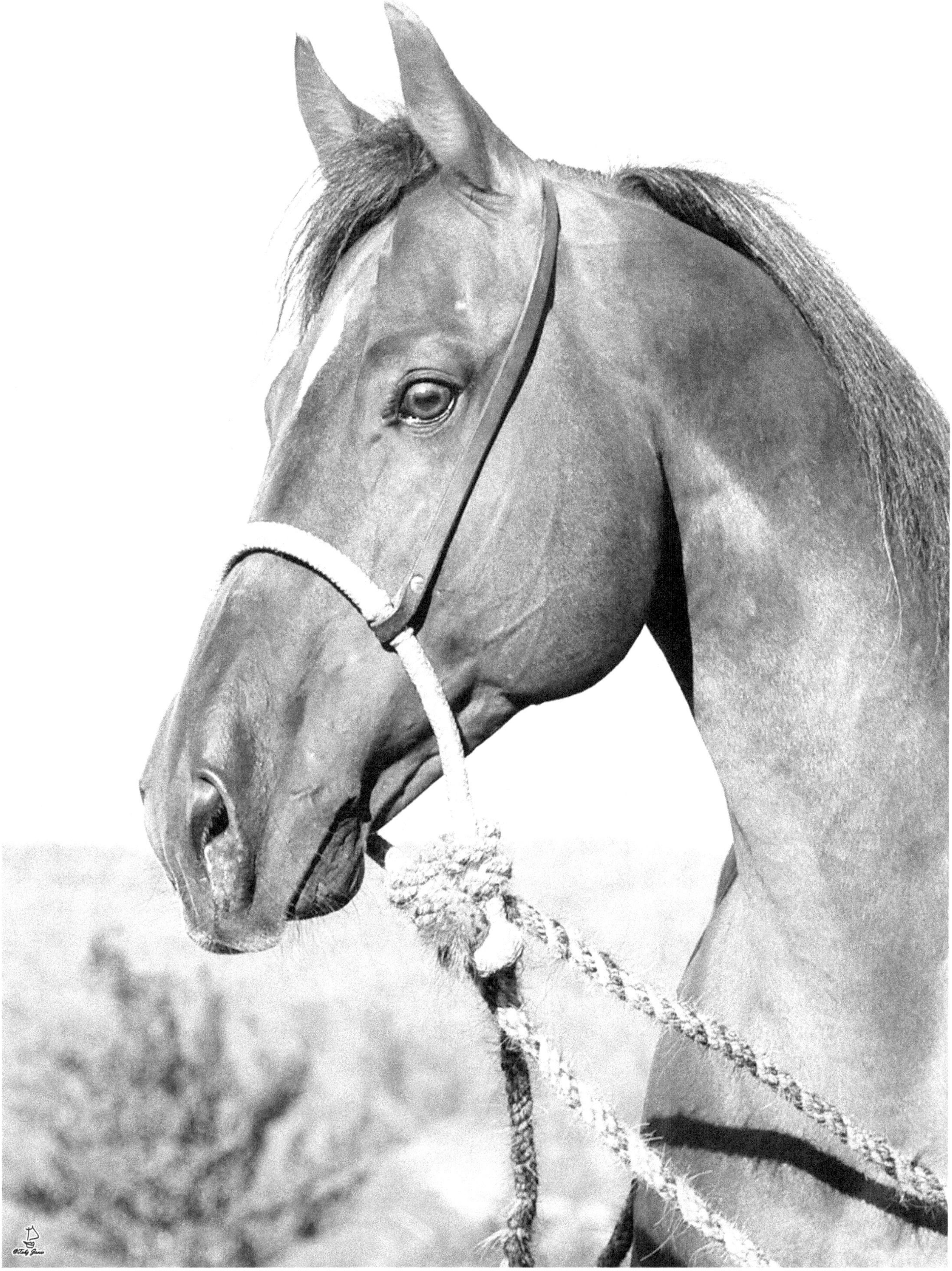

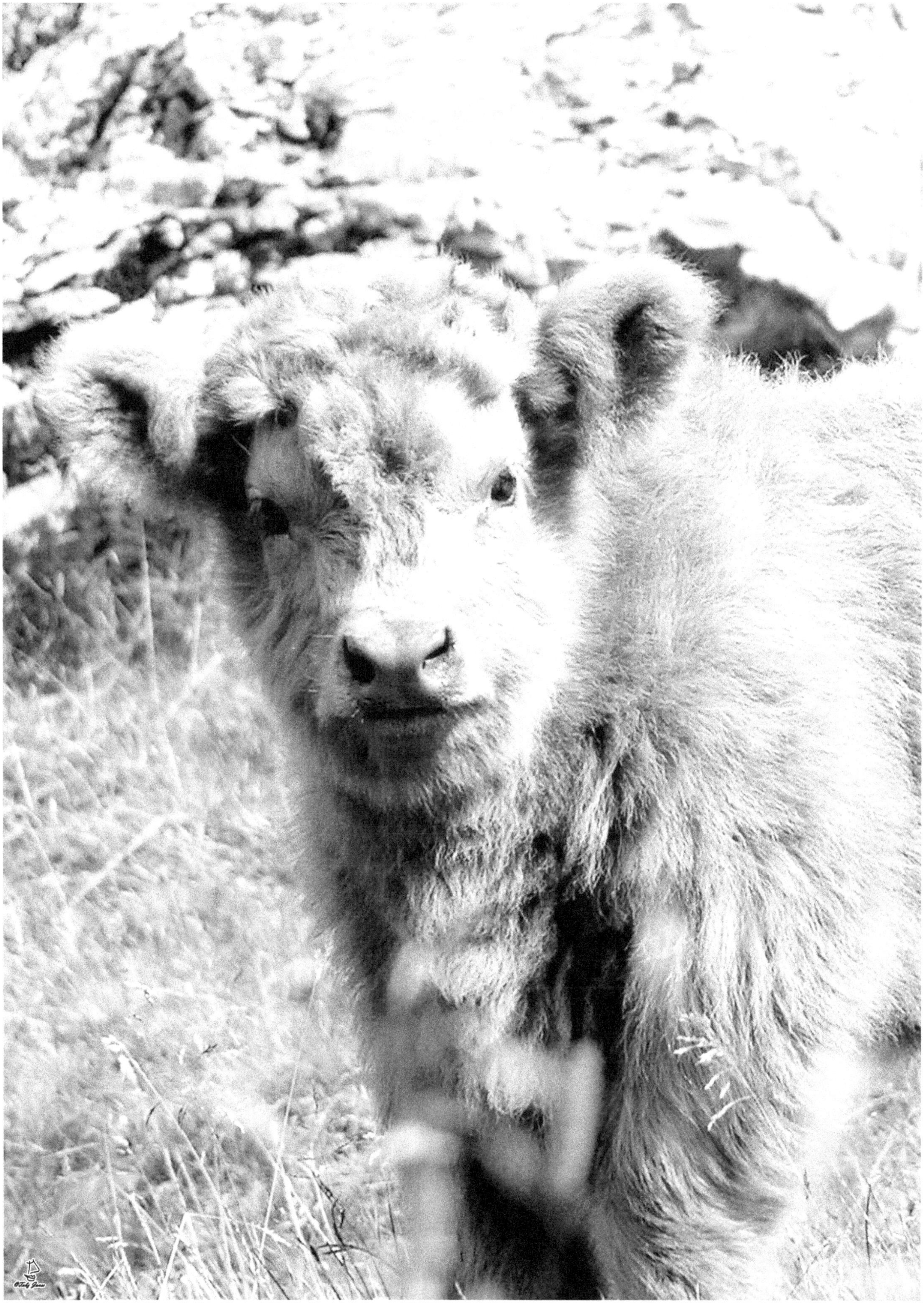

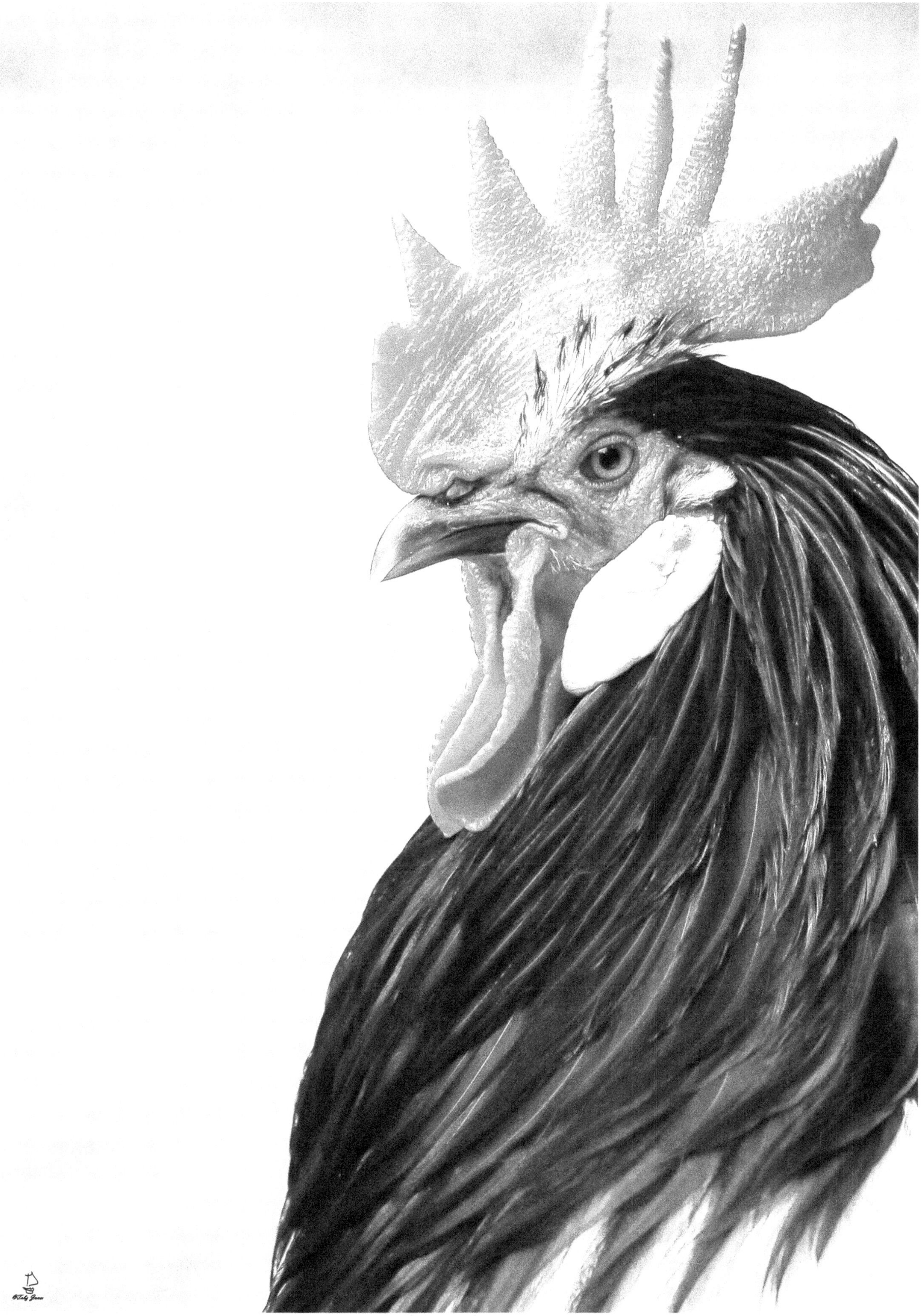

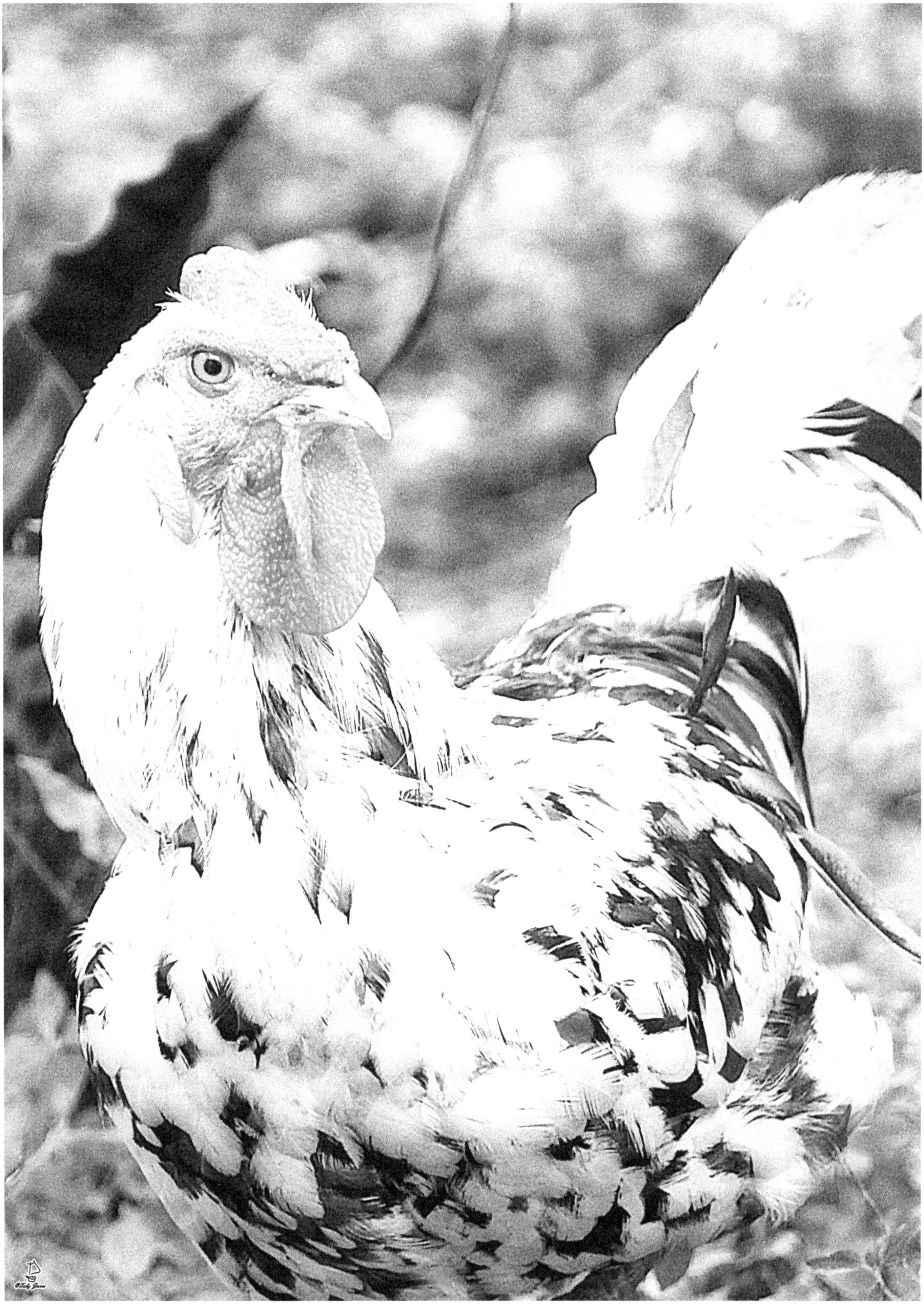

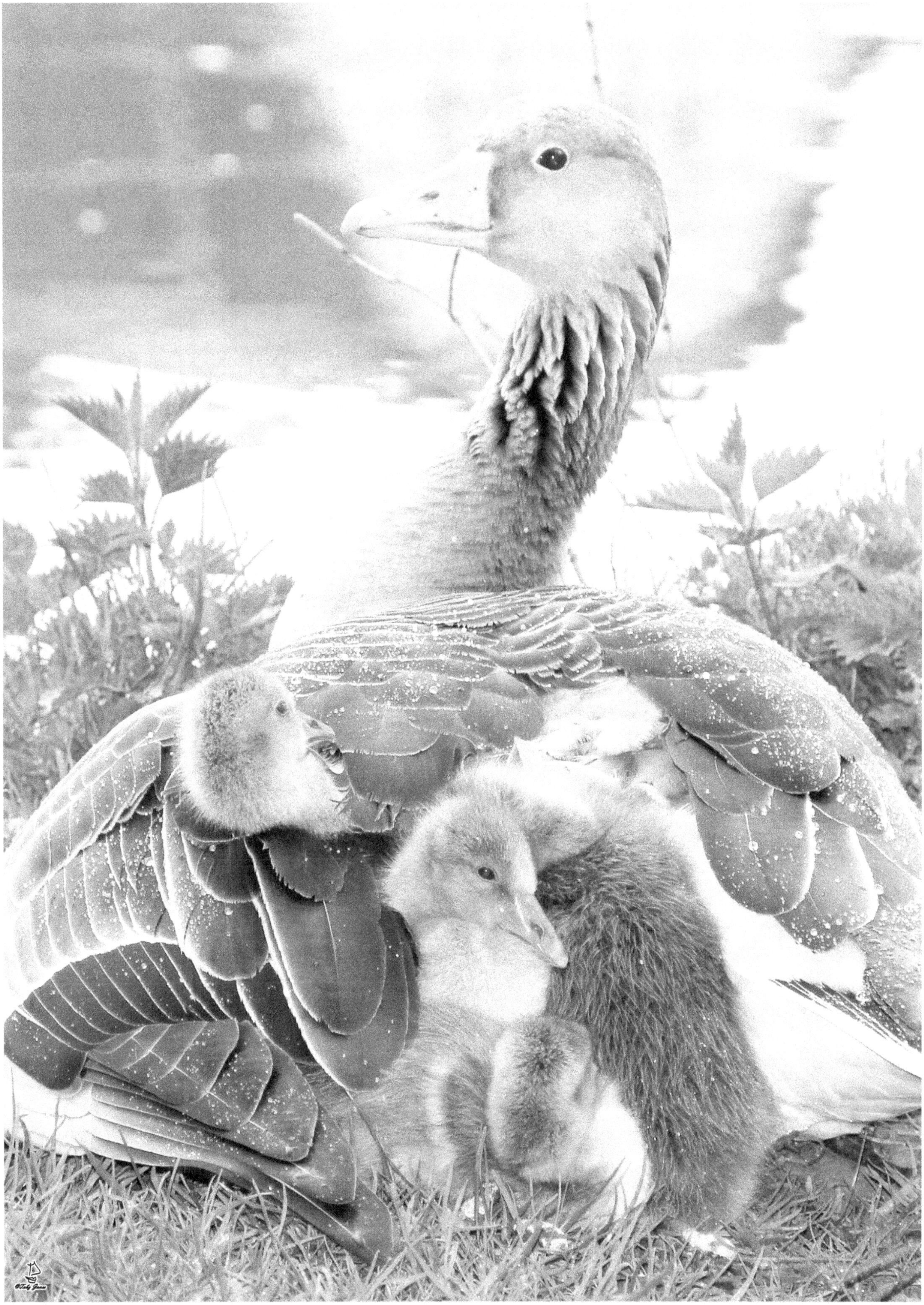

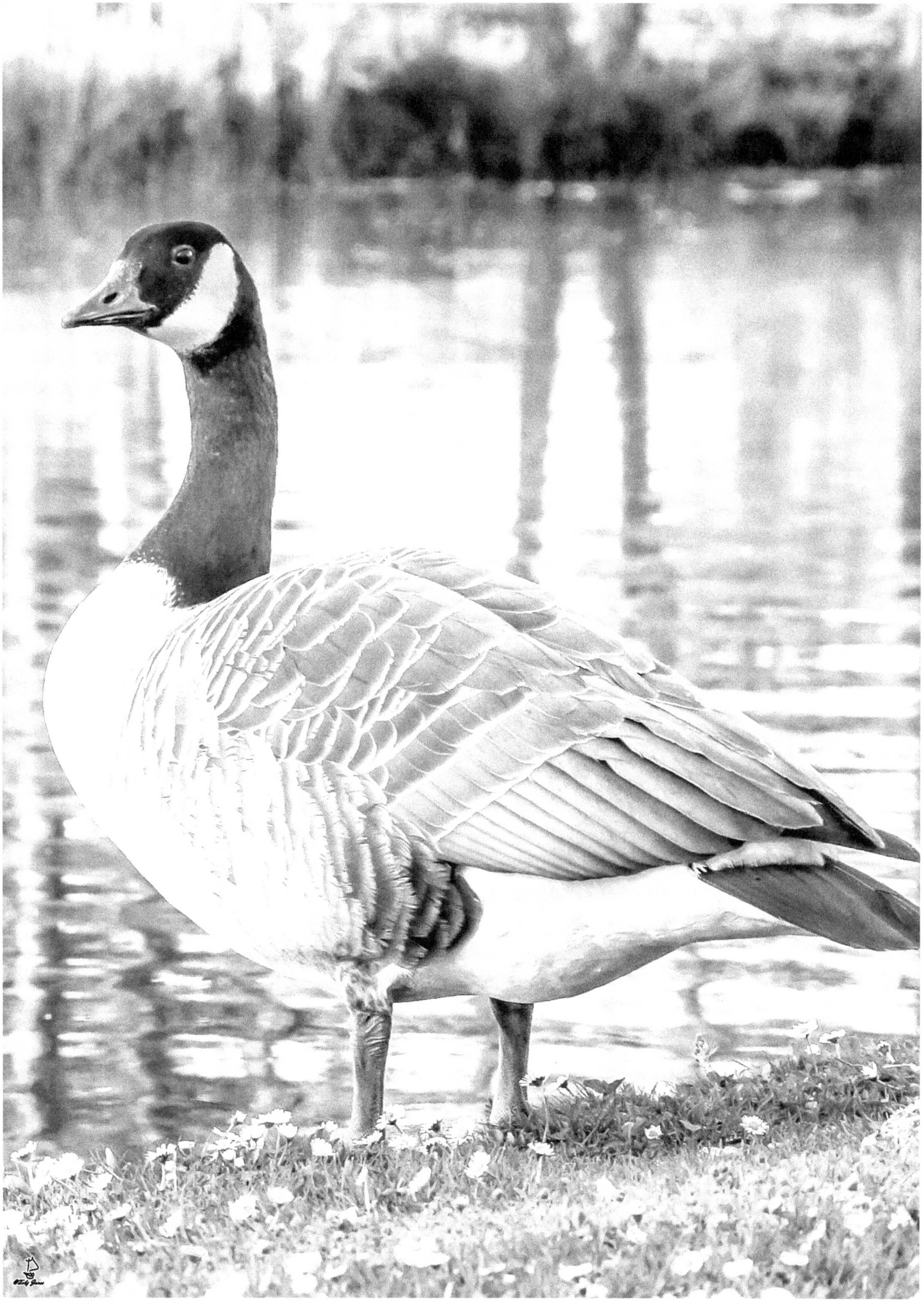

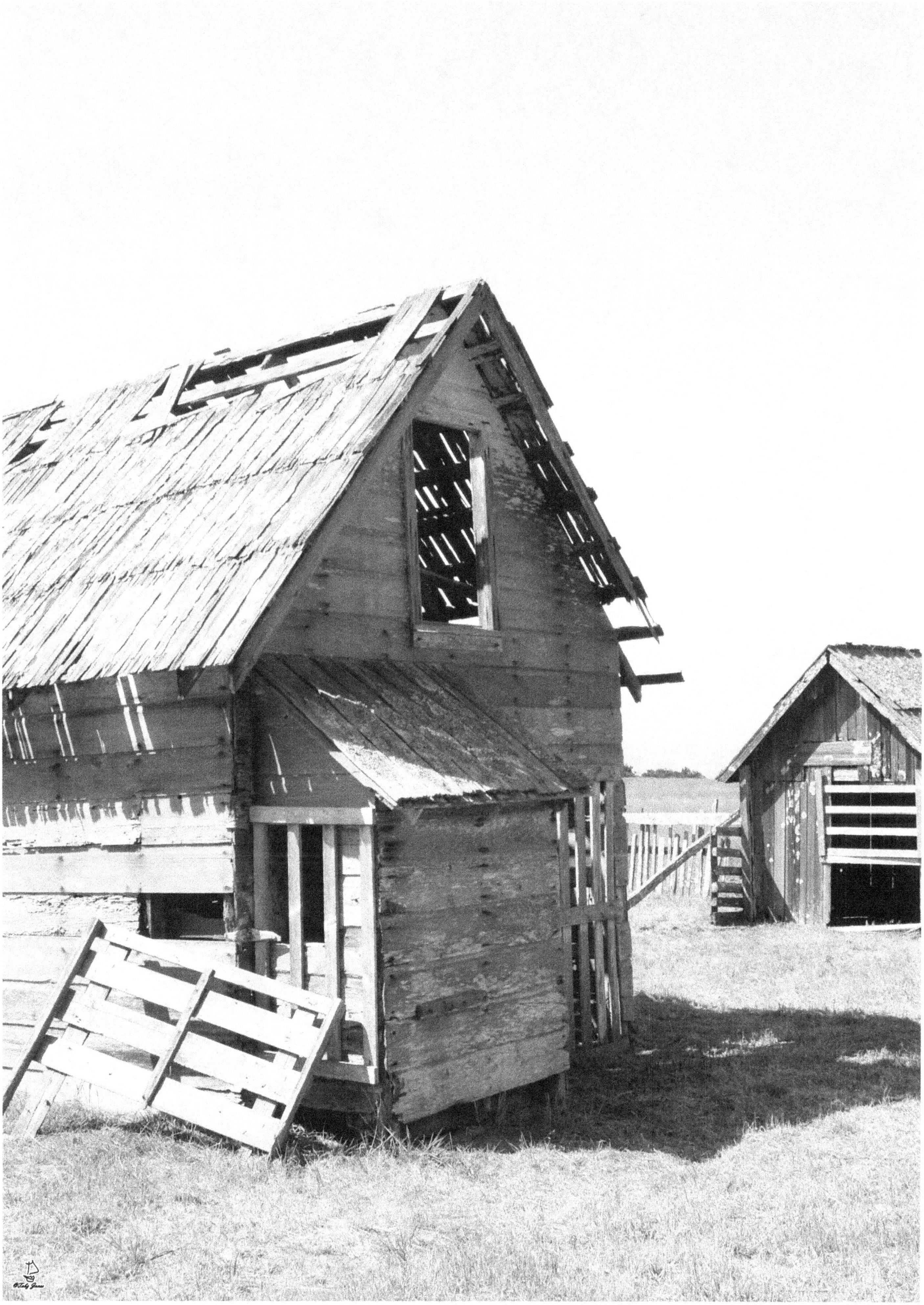

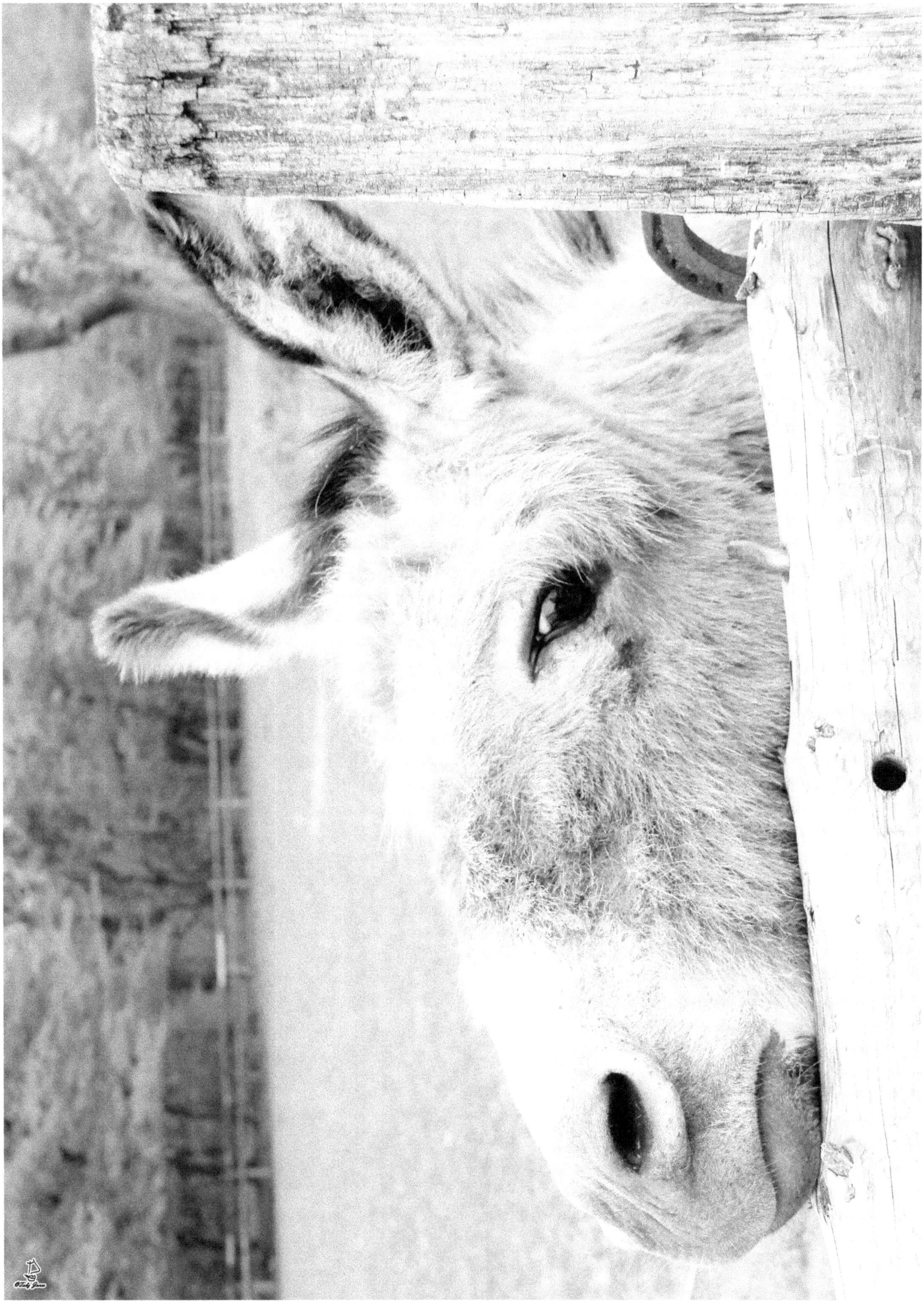

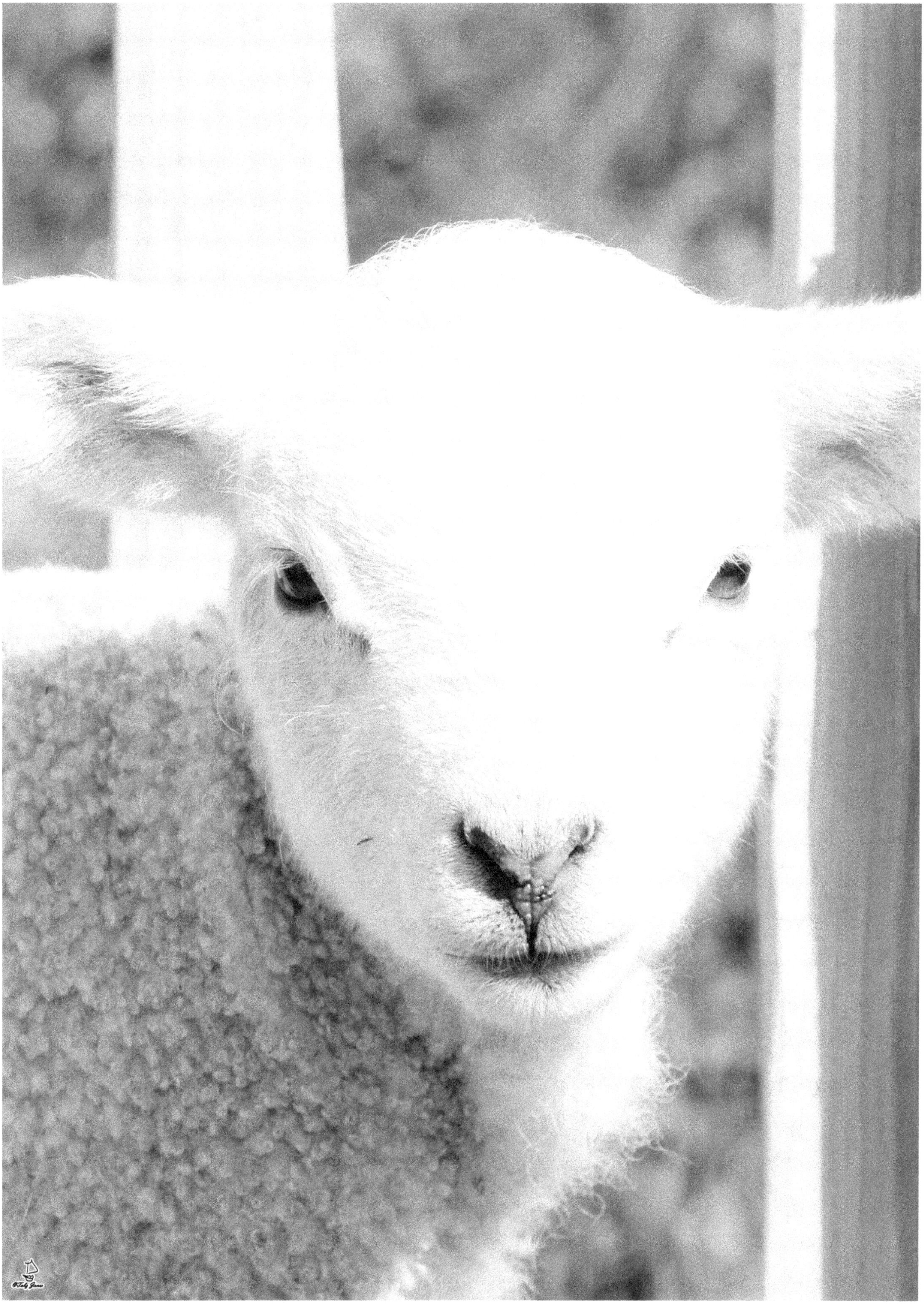

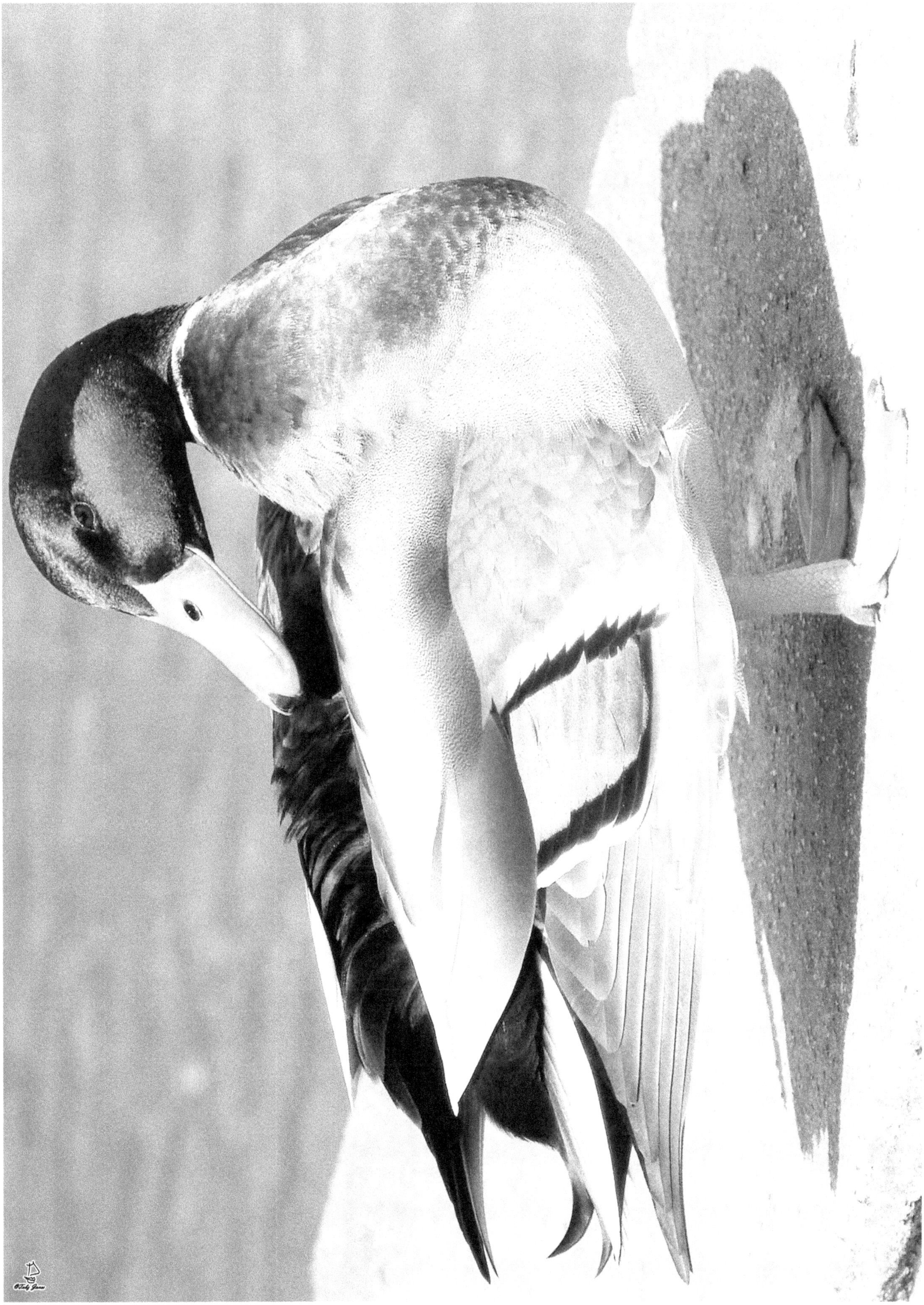

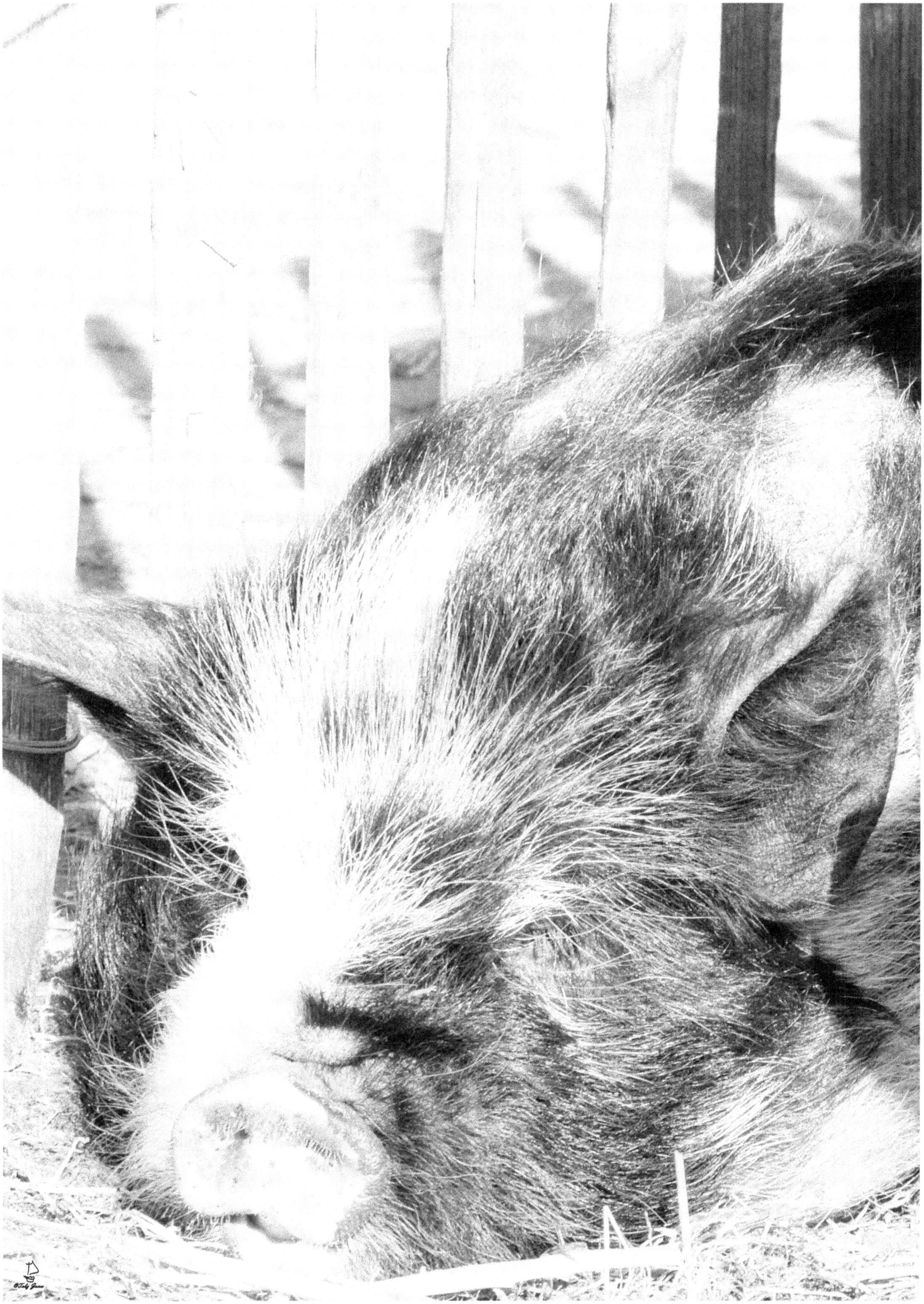

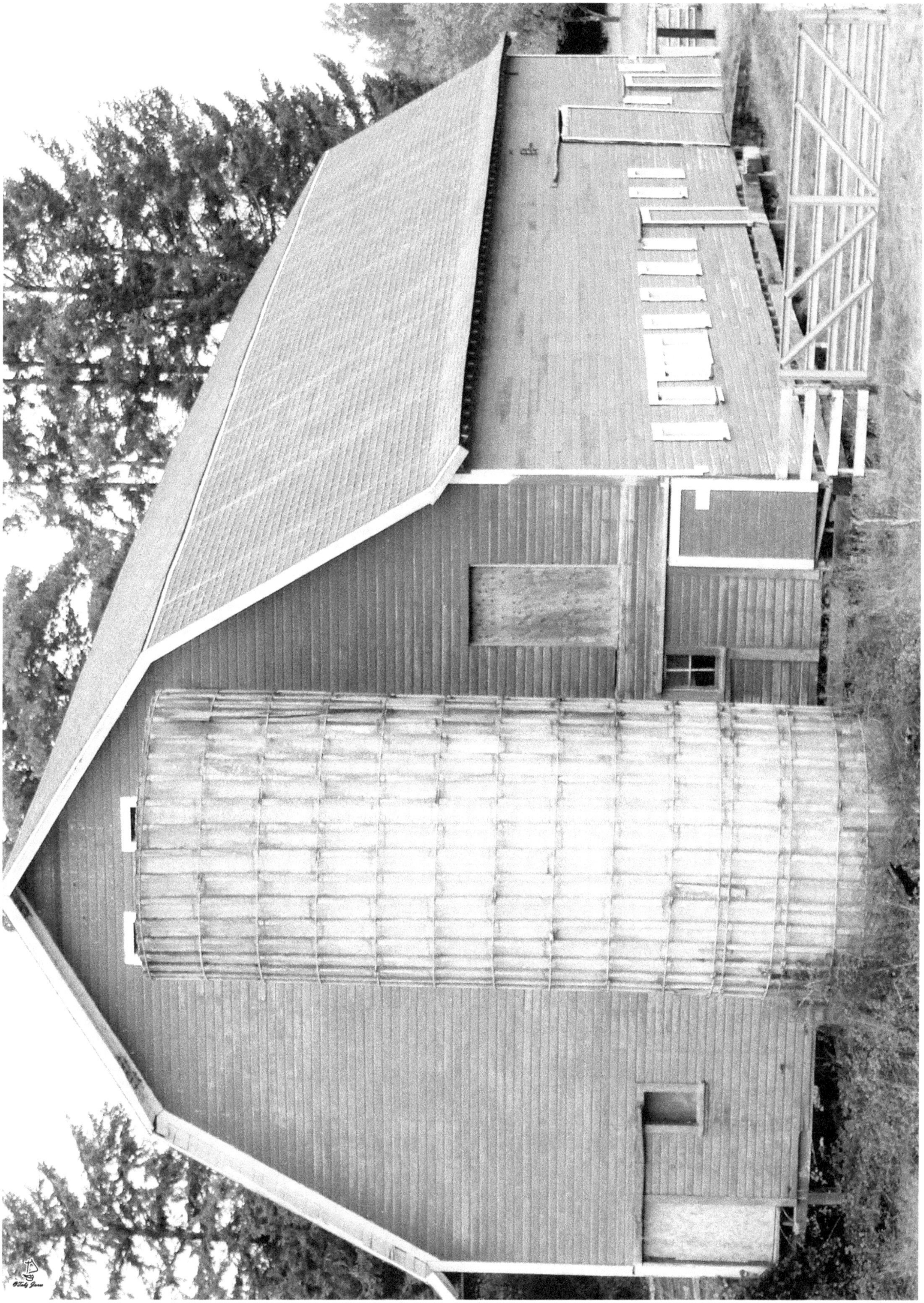

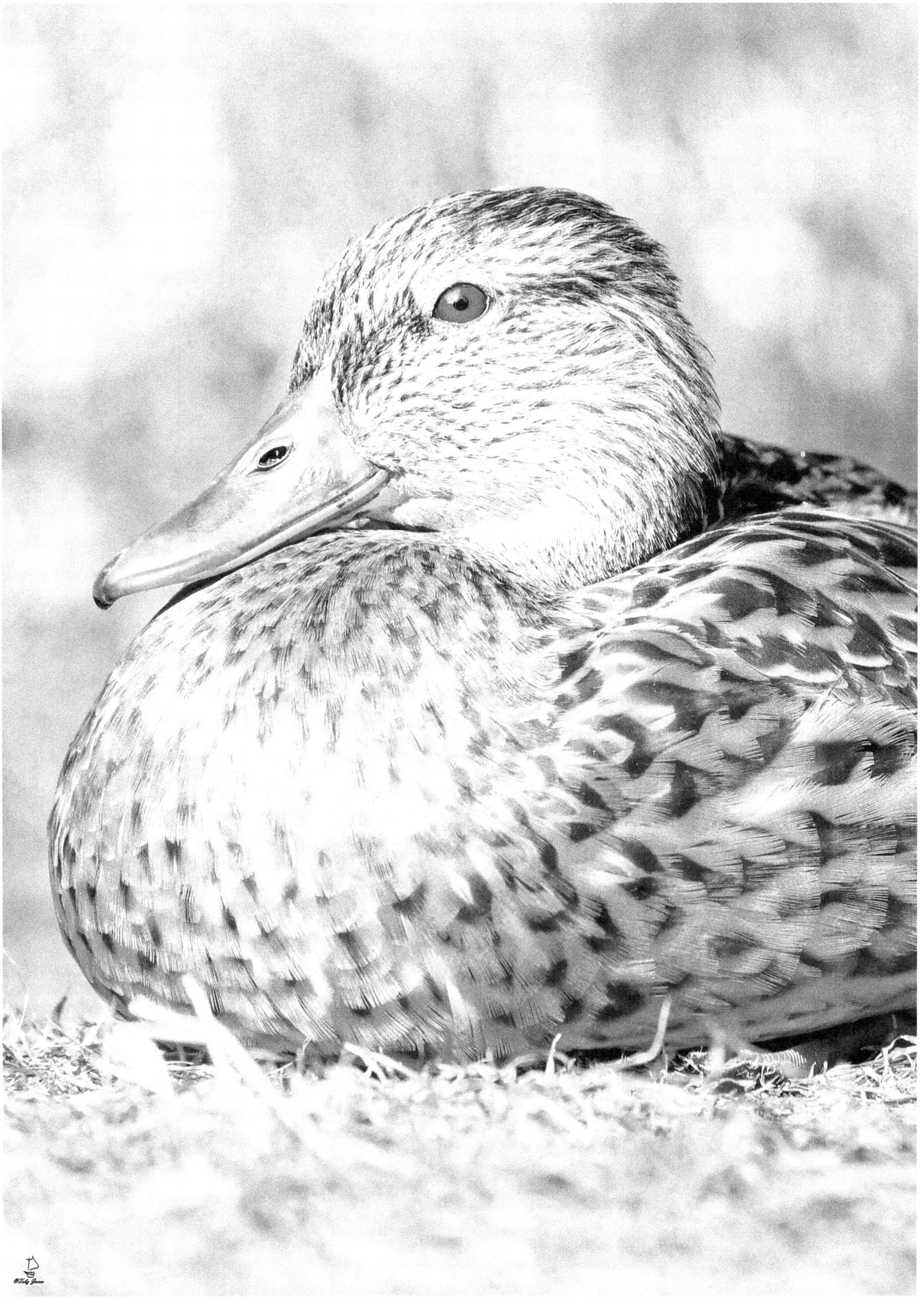

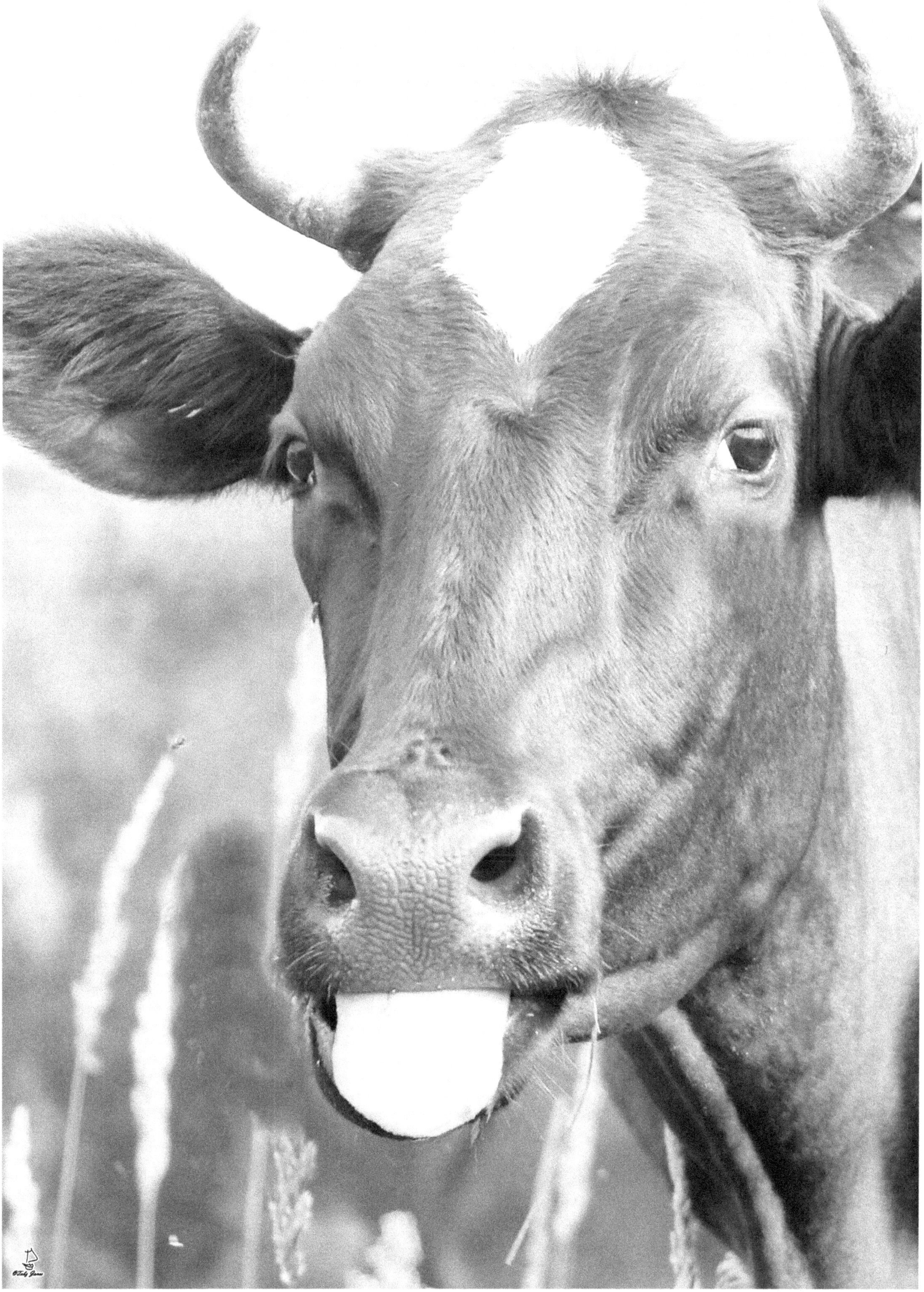

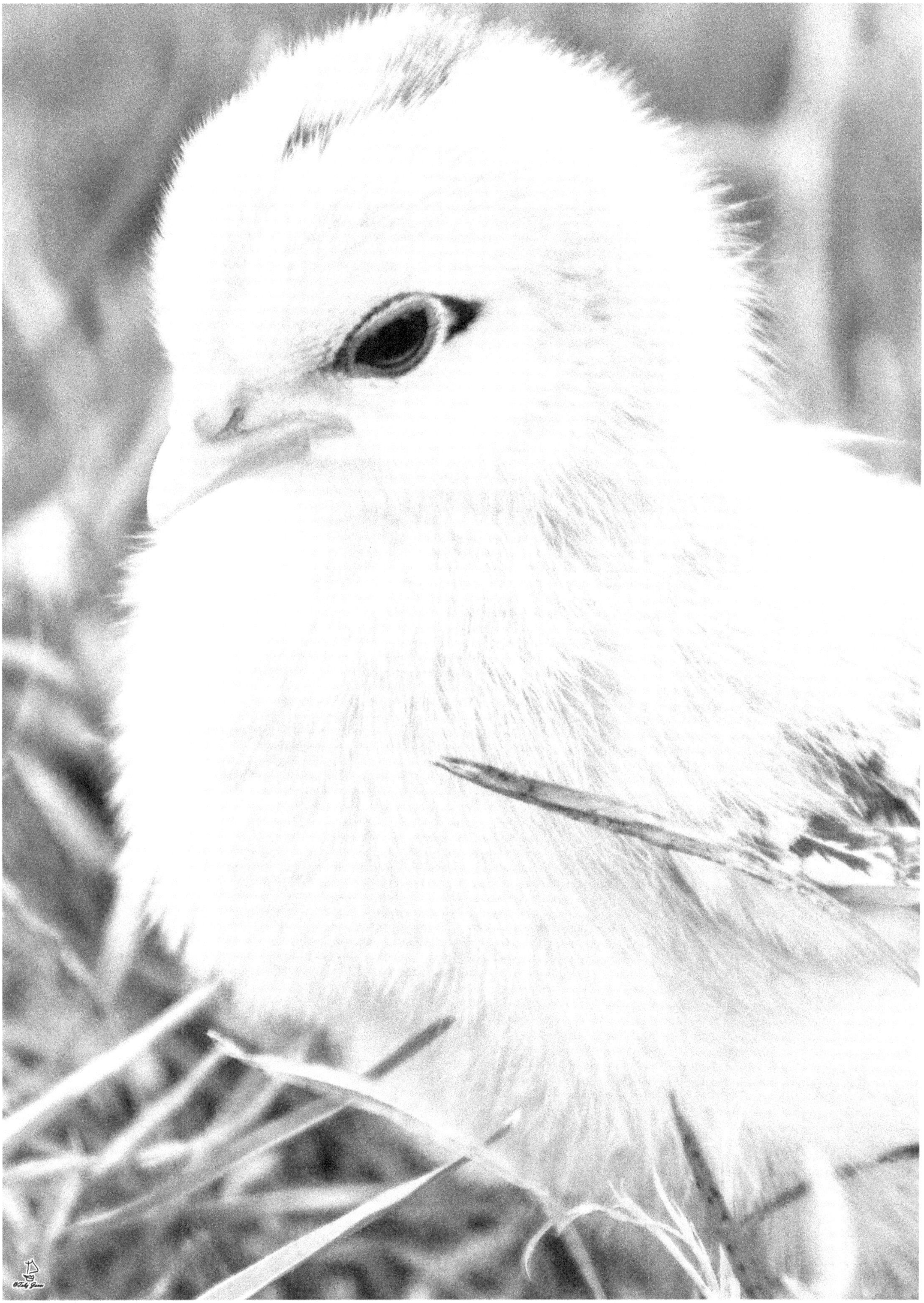

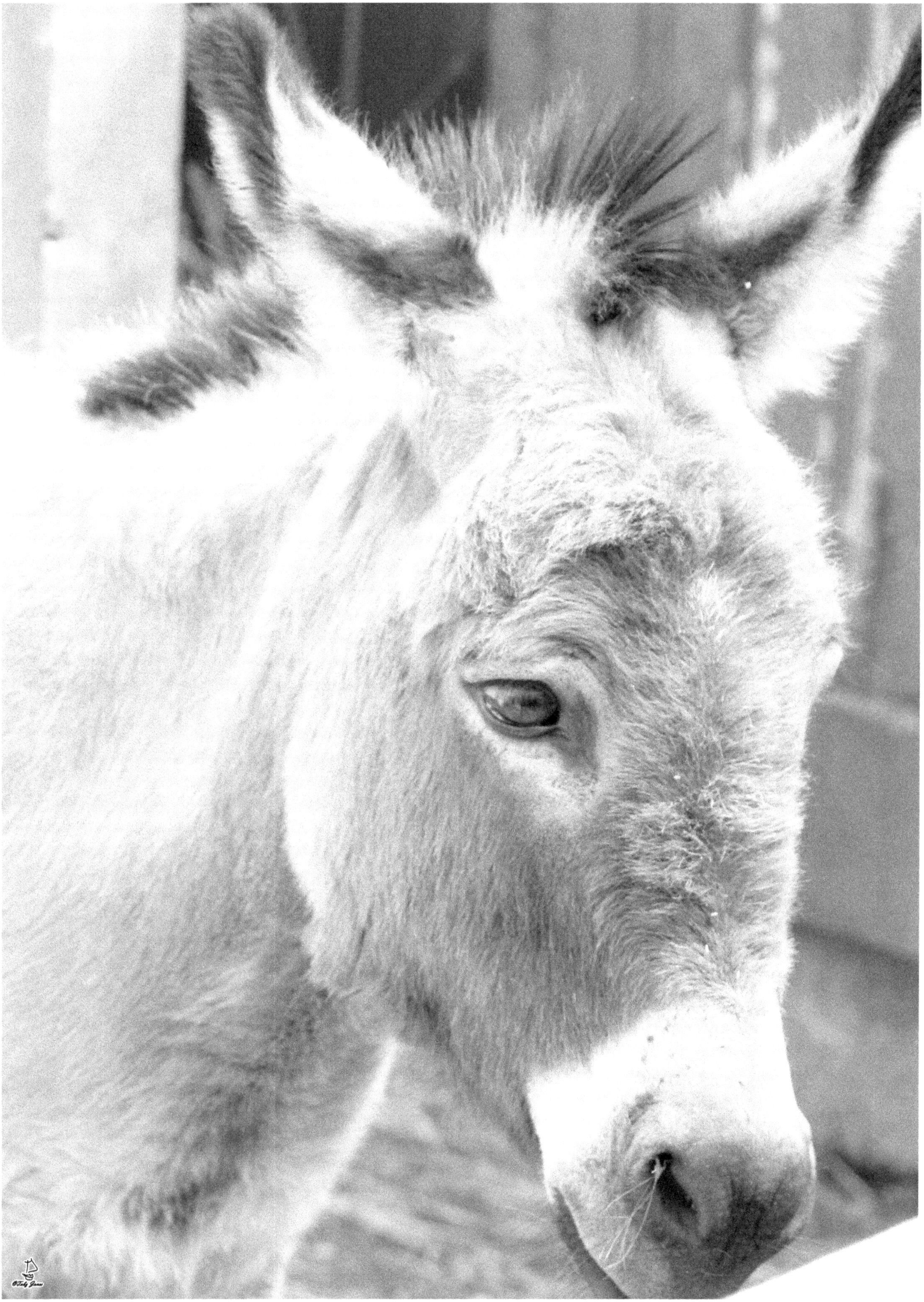

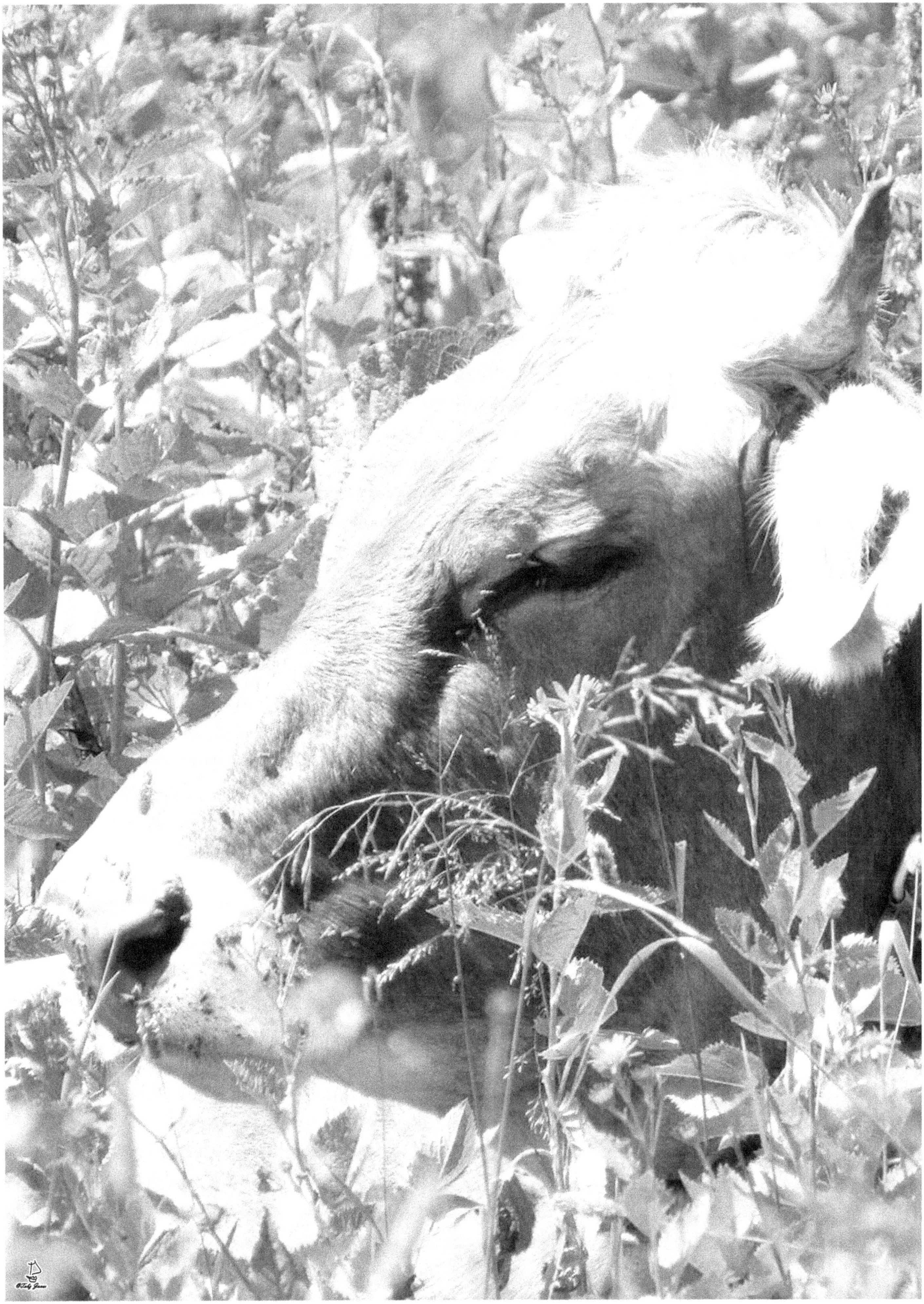

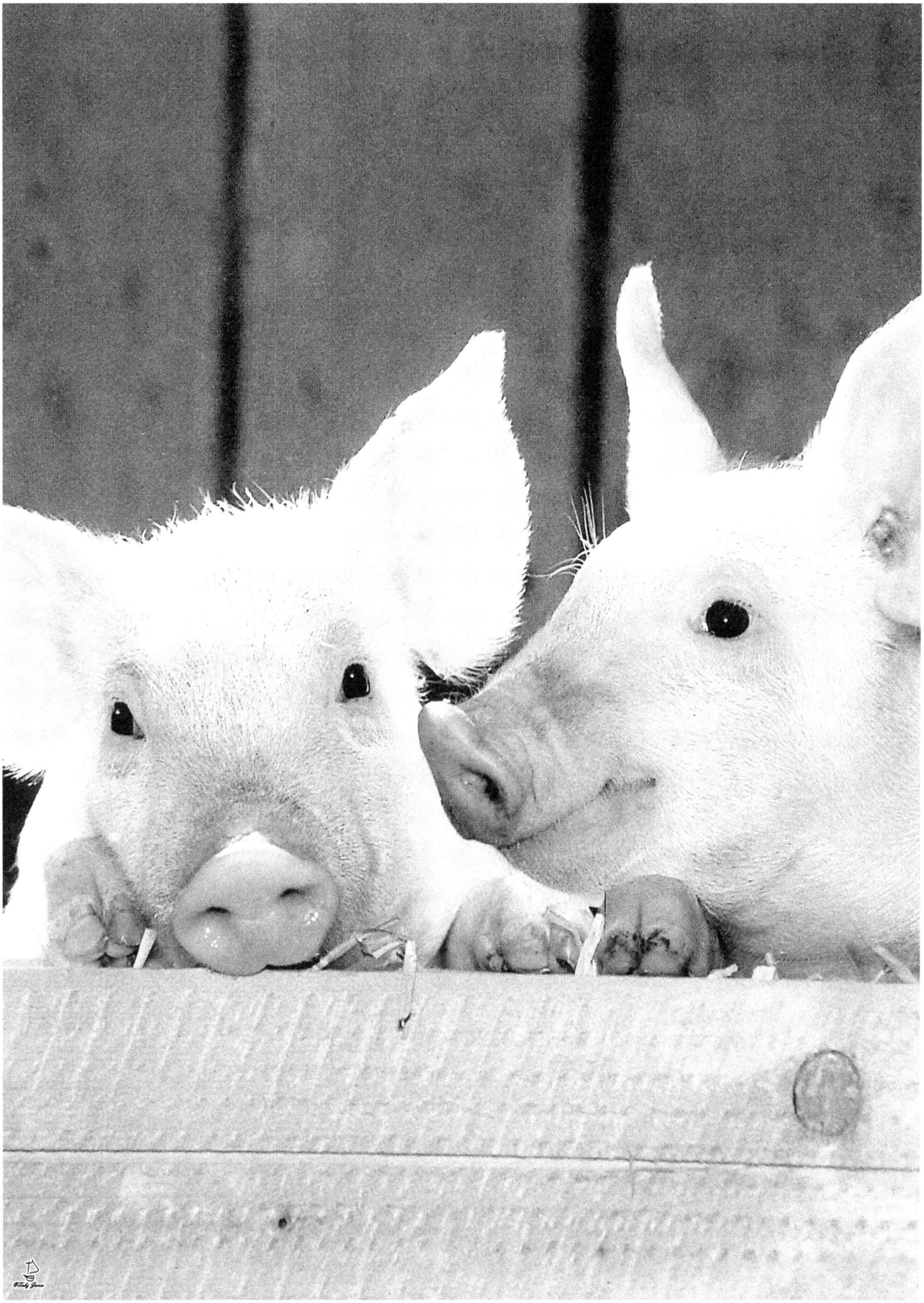

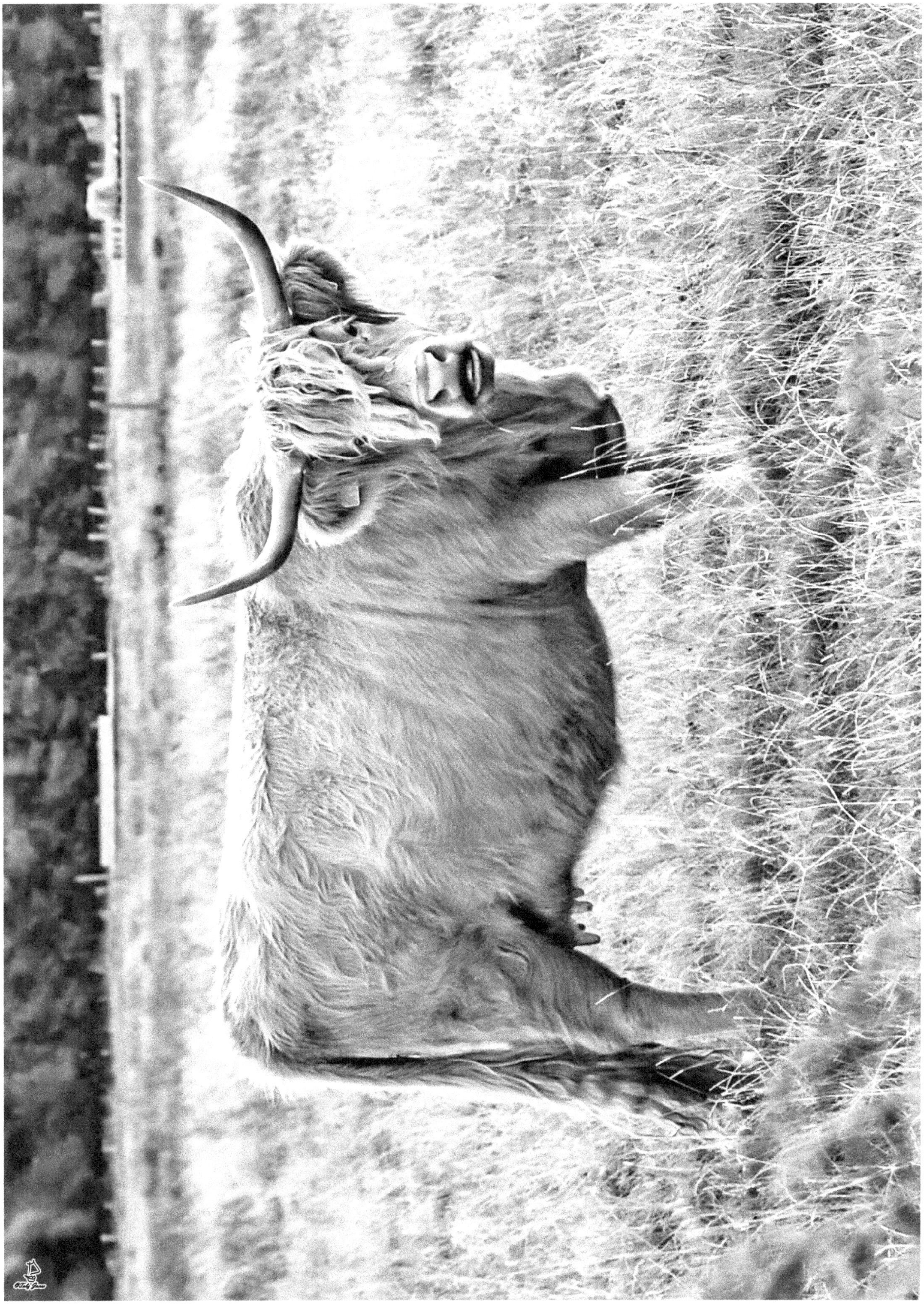

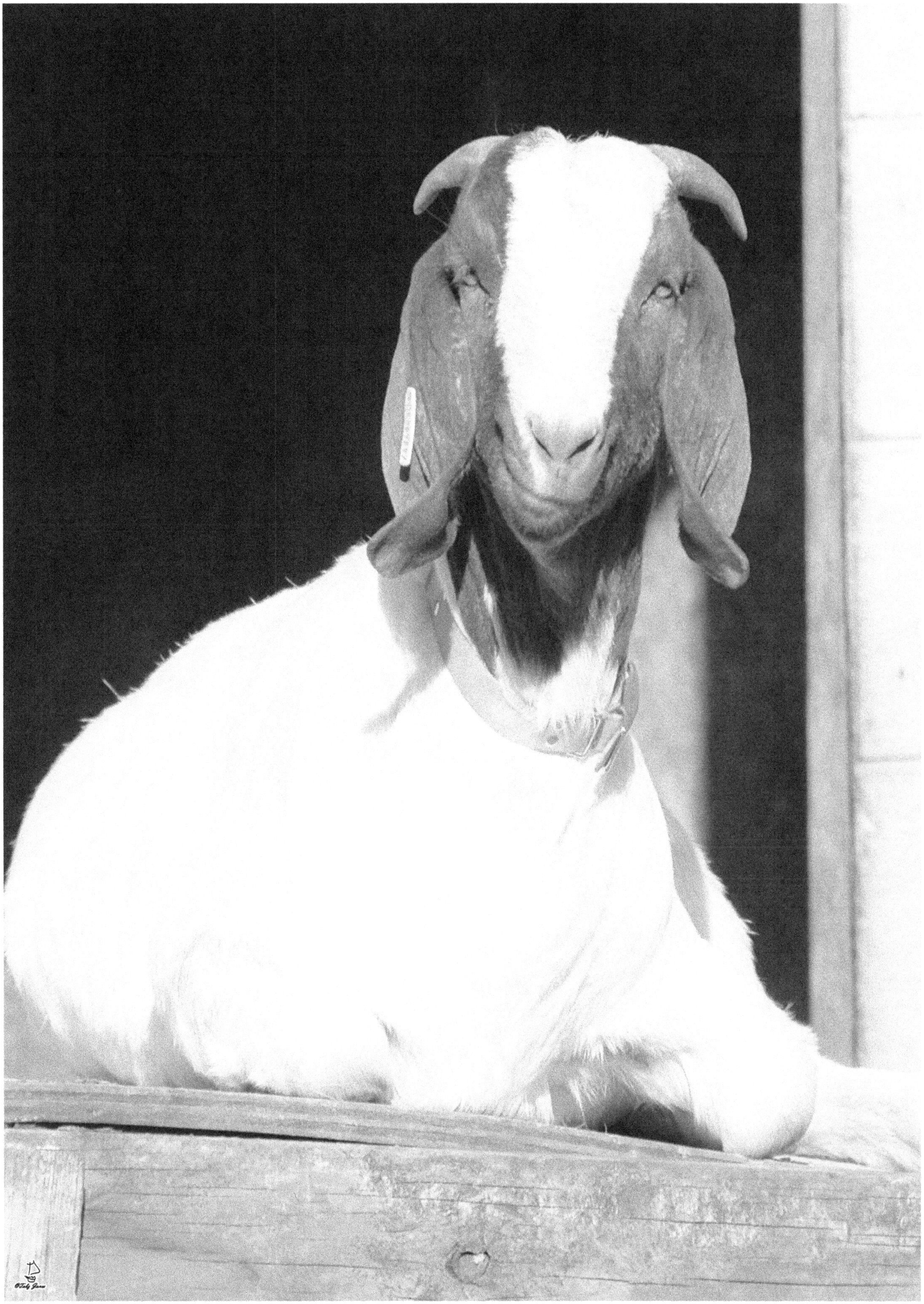

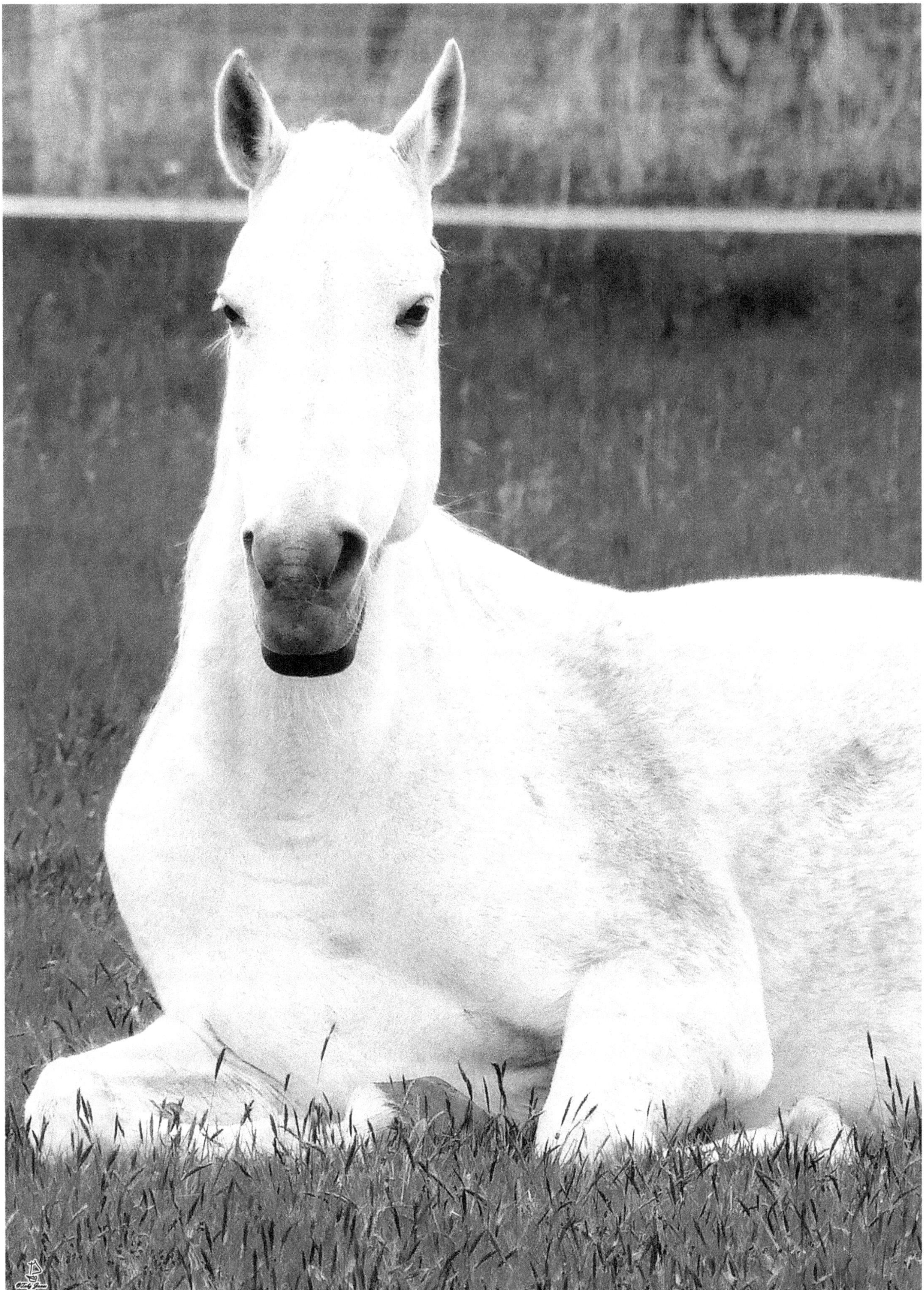

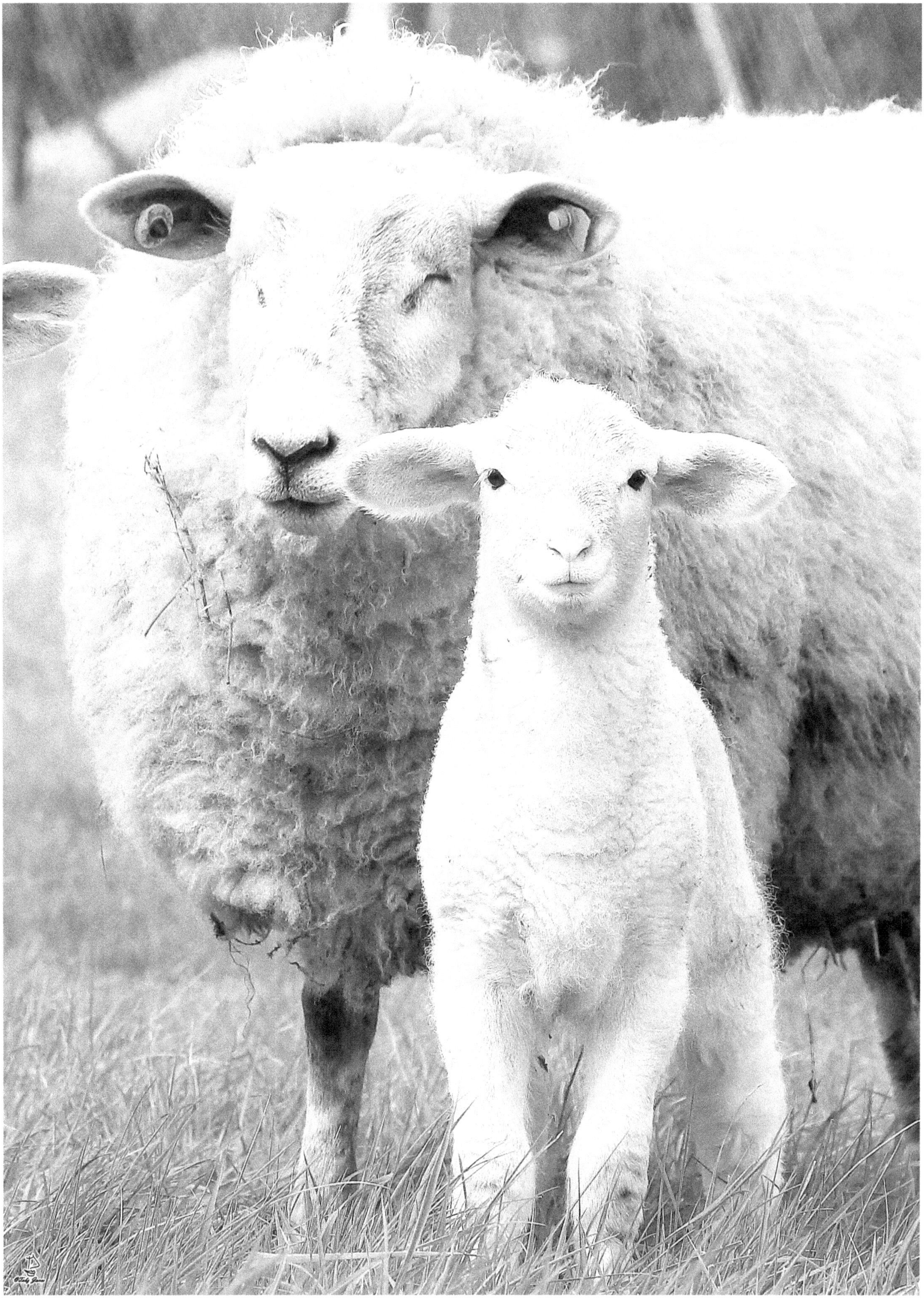

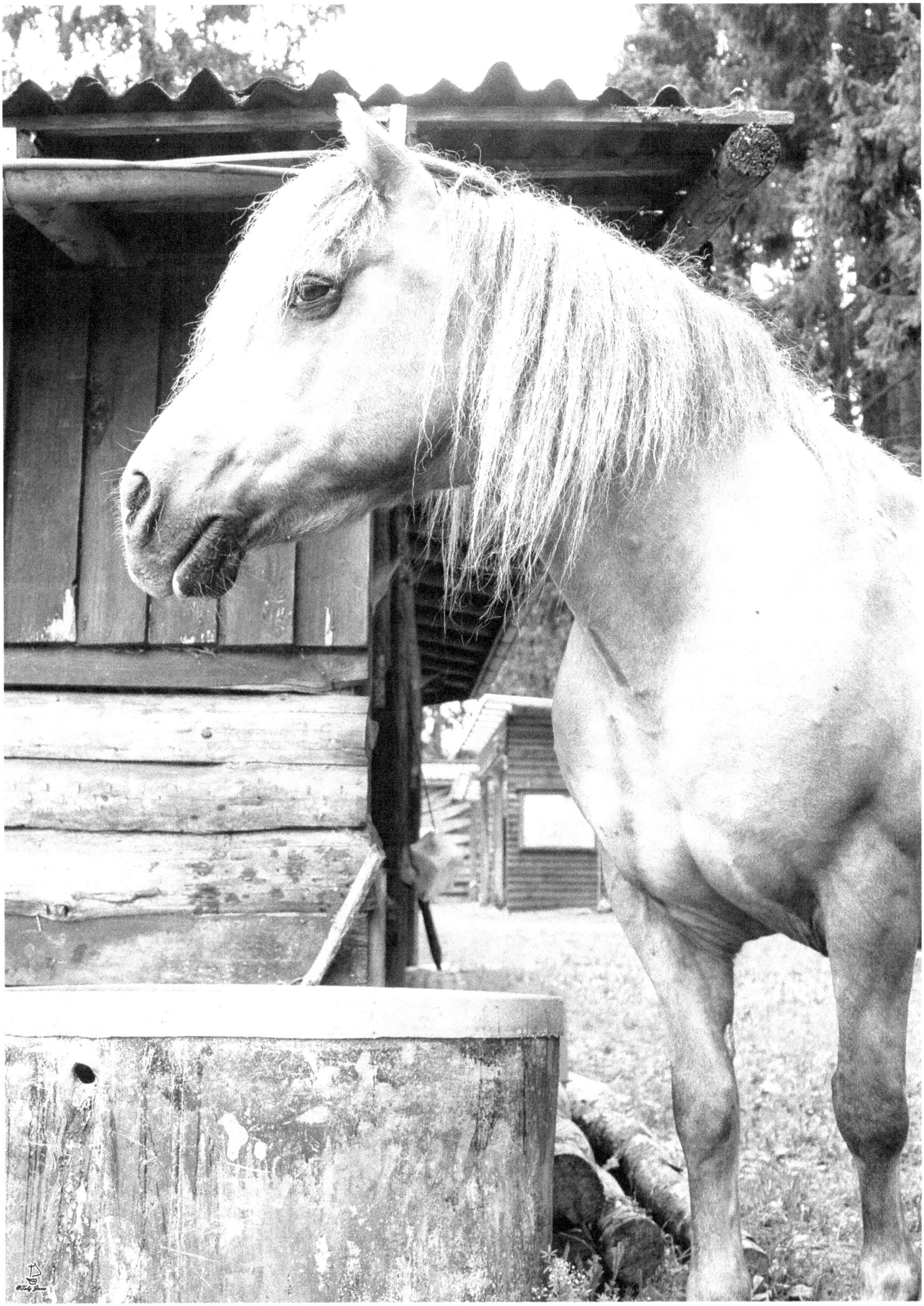

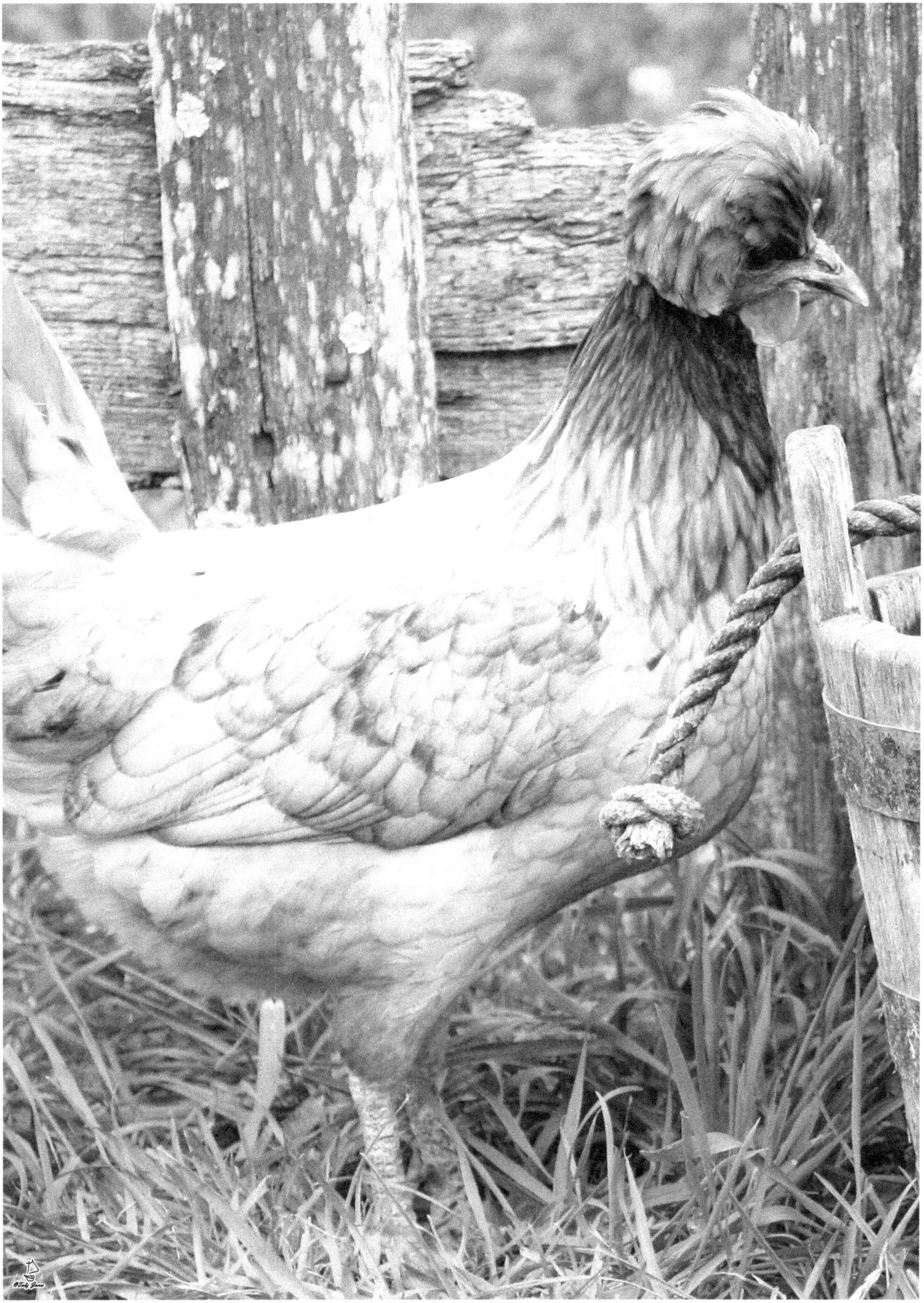

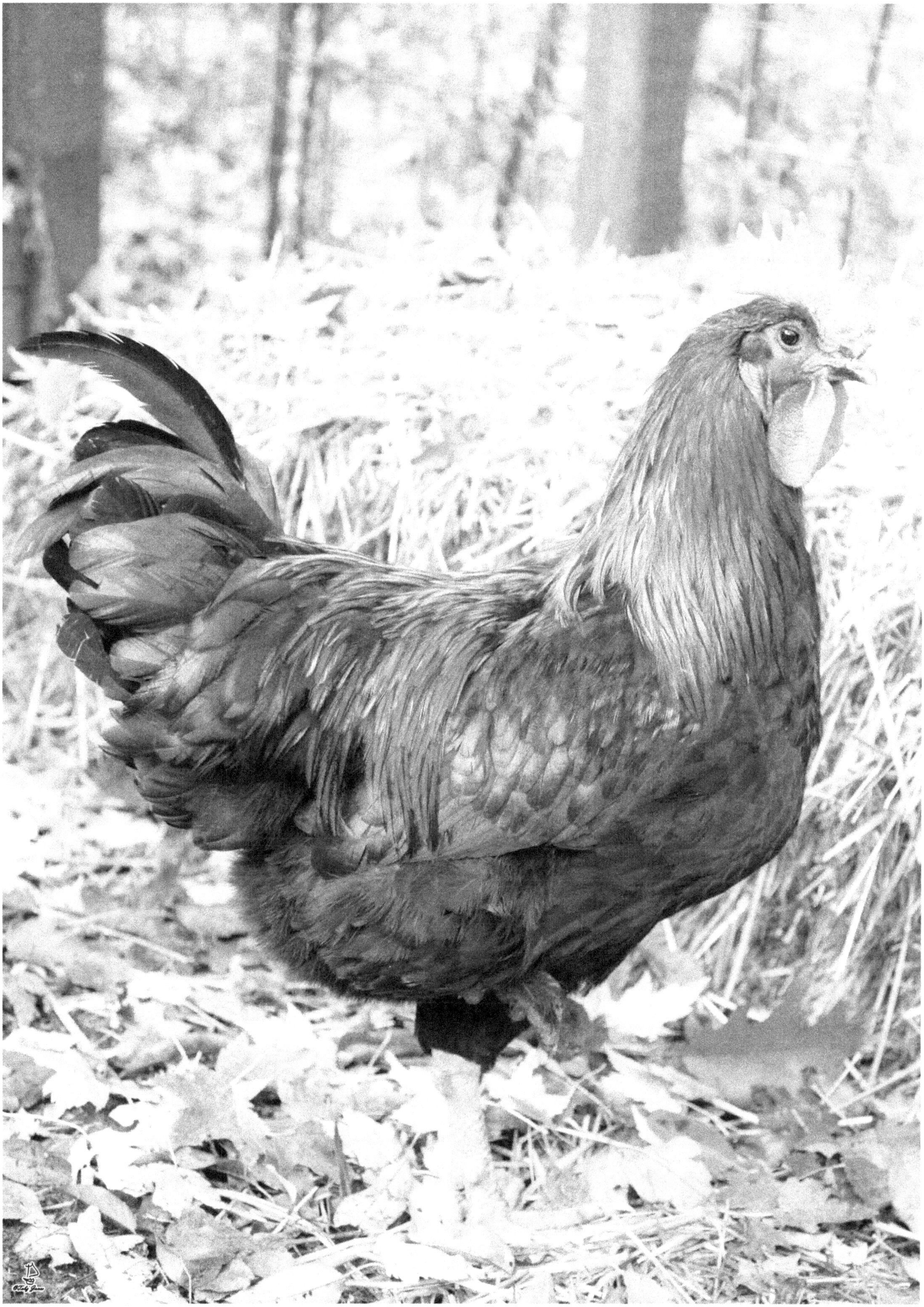

Thank you for your purchase!

To see the full catalog of my art, don't forget to stop by www.gothictoggs.net

www.ingramcontent.com/pod-product-compliance
Lightning Source LLC
Chambersburg PA
CBHW081302180526
45170CB00007B/2536
9781541347274